The Old Barn Book

The Old
Barn Book

Robin Langley Sommer

PROSPERO
B·O·O·K·S
A DIVISION OF CHARTWELL INC.

For Anne Hardee and Keith Warner, with love.

Published by Saraband Inc., PO Box 0032, Rowayton, CT 06853-0032, USA.

This edition produced for Prospero Books, a division of Chapters Inc.

Copyright © 1997 Saraband Inc.
Design © Ziga Design

ISBN: 1-887354-11-5

Printed in China

10 9 8 7 6 5 4 3 2 1

Contents

Introduction

Some of North America's most beautiful and historic buildings are seldom recognized as such. Located off the beaten path, the old barns of the United States and Canada are landmarks of national settlement and migration over a 400-year period. Their seasoned timbers, sturdy roofs, varied shapes and styles of ornamentation are passing into history now, but some fine examples are still working buildings, and others have been restored for reuse or preservation as pioneer and agricultural museums. Ontario's Upper Canada Village, for example, has various landmarks of vernacular architecture that were moved to prevent their destruction in the widening of the St. Lawrence River Ship Canal. In the United States, Colonial Williamsburg, Virginia, and the Shaker Hancock Museum in Massachusetts provide glimpses into our rural past.

The following pages explore both the European prototypes of North American barns and the adaptations that fitted them for use in the New World. Livestock shelters and granaries had been built in Europe for more than a thousand years, but much of what we know about them has been gleaned from medieval manuscripts and paintings. Especially noteworthy are paintings of the Nativity, transposed from the historic cave-stable of the Holy Land to the familiar timber-frame shelters of Germany, Italy, and the Low Countries. In the early fifteenth century, for example, Renaissance artist Giovanni di Paolo

Opposite: *An Amish buggy driver and his Standardbred horse make their way past a whitewashed banked barn in New Holland, Pennsylvania.*

Below: *A hayrack adjoins a typical three-bay barn in Ohio, which has been enlarged by the right-angle extension (with red roof) visible at left.*

depicted the adoration of the Magi in a Sienese landscape, with a byre (cow stall) of squared timbers and woven sticks, roofed with thatching lashed to a series of poles. This type of construction would be carried bodily to the New World, but there the lack of suitable thatching materials soon led to new types of roofing, including bark slabs, boards, and shingles.

According to Eric Sloane, the author of *An Age of Barns*, it was the settlers of North America who developed the integrated barn, combining hay and grain storage and stalls for livestock. Originally, they stored their harvests in covered holes, as did many northeastern Woodlands tribes. However, "By 1770 (according to *Kalm's Travels*), the ground storage hole had become a building—the American having originated the idea of putting the farm complex under one roof." Kalm reported to his European readers that "In the northern states of America, the farmers generally use barns for stabling their horses and cattle; so that among them, a barn is both a cornhouse or grange, and a stable."

The following pages illustrate the major kinds of North American barns, including the English three-bay style with wagon doors on the broad side; the nearly square Dutch barn with doors at the gable ends; and the German or Swiss banked barn, with livestock in the lower level and threshing floor and hay mows above. The latter were usually built into a hillside or bank, providing easy access to the wagon entrances at the upper level. Many included a forebay, which overhung the lower level to provide shade or shelter for the animals and grain storage adjacent to the threshing floor. Before the advent of hay baling, hay was stored loose in the mows, sometimes reaching rafter height. Thus we see few windows at the gable ends of old barns except at the topmost level.

Construction materials varied according to local availability, from fieldstone and brick made of clay to timber-frame with board cladding (the commonest form), and notched logs joined at the corners—the familiar log cabin introduced by Swedish and German settlers. Timber was so plentiful in the New World that most homesteaders built houses, barns, and outbuildings of wood. Trees suitable for framing were cut down and allowed to season for at least a year, then hewn into squared beams. Framing timbers had projecting tongues, called tenons, and notches (mortises) into which the tenons were pegged securely. Whole sections, called "bents," were preassembled on the ground, then raised onto the foundation by the whole community, working with sixteen-foot pikes and a derrick. Once the bents (usually four or five) were up, a horizontal timber called the plate was inserted to connect the tops of the outside posts and support the rafters. At this point, all the neighbors went home, and the farmer and his workers did the time-consuming job of adding siding and roofing to the newly framed barn. Inevitably, there were accidents, as seen in this picturesque epitaph, quoted in *An Age of Barns*:

JOHN MOODY, 1801
Killed at noon on the fourth of November,
in raising his barn he was hit by a timber.
Be ye also ready for in such an hour
cometh the Son of Man.

Certain types of wood were favored for specific uses: durable oak for framing barns and houses; lightweight, weather-resistant pine for siding, ship masts, and furniture; rot-resistant cedar for fencing, tubs, and pails. Pliable hickory was fashioned into barrel hoops and baskets, and chestnut bark was favored for shingling. Even stone buildings had wooden armatures, to keep the walls from spreading with changes in temperature. In very cold climates, frost formed on the inner walls of the stone barn, posing a threat to the health and comfort of livestock. The timber-frame shelter, or the log barn, chinked for the winter with moss or straw, provided more warmth.

A number of religious sects, including the Mennonites, Amish, and Shakers, had an influence on North American agriculture out of all proportion to their numbers. Conscientious, cooperative, and industrious, they set a high standard of craftsmanship in their close-knit communities that was widely admired and emulated. The Mennonites originated in Switzerland during the Reformation era and took their name from a former priest, Menno Simons, who

Opposite: *Top to bottom, three stages in the construction of an early twentieth-century log-and-frame prairie barn built near Baljennie, Saskatchewan.*

Left: *Massive timber framing rises 48 feet to the two-stage roof of this octagonal cattle barn near Gagetown, Michigan.*

Above: *An immaculate connected barn in Queens County, Prince Edward Island, shows the saltbox style: a long sloped roof that "focuses the weather" on the north side.*

organized the Anabaptists—Christians opposed to infant baptism and the unity of church and state. Persecuted in Europe, many of the Mennonites emigrated to the future United States and Canada.

Eastern Pennsylvania was widely settled by German immigrants known as the Pennsylvania Dutch (derived from the word *Deutsch*, meaning German). They included the Amish—Mennonite separatists led by Bishop Jacob Amman, who formed still-flourishing communities in Berks and Lancaster Counties. Some of the Amish later settled in Ohio and Indiana, where they remain today.

The Shakers, formed among the English Quakers in 1797, were so called because they trembled with religious fervor during their services, which included liturgical dancing. They sought material and spiritual perfection in their celibate communities, building barns and crafting furniture and other household goods of rare simplicity and beauty. The barn at Hancock Shaker Village, Massachusetts, is one of the finest surviving round stone barns on the continent. Sadly, the Shaker communities have been all but extinguished, since they depended entirely upon converts to continue their tradition.

Several distinguished but atypical North American barns deserve mention here because they do not fit within the usual categories. One is the architect-designed complex at Shelburne Farms, Vermont, originally the model farm and agricultural estate of William Seward Webb and Lila Vanderbilt Webb. The original Breeding Barn designed by Robert H. Robertson, was more than 400 feet long, 100 feet wide, and 2 stories high—the largest barn in the United States when it was completed in 1891. The nearby Dairy Barn, also designed by Robertson, was used to stable brood mares before it was converted to house a herd of up to 50 Jersey cows. The 5-story Farm Barn, headquarters for the estate, had a 2-acre courtyard and a 1,500-ton storage capacity in the main hayloft. The entire complex was acquired from the Shelburne Museum in 1994 and is being developed by Shelburne Farms as an independent, nonprofit educational organization.

An exceptionally large barn was built by the Shakers in New Lebanon, New York, just before the Civil War. Some 300 feet long and 5 stories high, this stone structure survives, but the original flat roofline was altered to peaked form when leakage became a problem. A similar, appro-

Left: *Another beautiful Canadian barn shows its colors under peaked and gambrel rooflines in the Maritime Provinces.*

priately named "Big Barn" was constructed at Lyons Falls, New York, in 1860. The hay mow was 4 stories high. Unfortunately, it has been demolished, along with the huge W. T. Smith Ranch barn built near Leader, Saskatchewan, before World War I. It measured 400 feet long, 128 feet wide, and 60 feet high, in keeping with the vast plains of western Canada.

Whether grand or modest in scale, weathered gray or brightly painted, rectangular, round, or polygonal, alone on the prairie or nestled on a hillside, the old barn retains its hold on our collective memory. It is hoped that this book may draw us back in time to an era when life was more arduous, but perhaps more serene than it is today.

Below: *A "double-decker" unpainted barn and outbuildings in rural New York State.*

Colonial Influences

✤ —— ✤

North America's first region of extensive settlement was the Eastern Seaboard, where vernacular architecture, including the earliest barns, was shaped by European prototypes. Early Colonial styles can still be traced in the old barns of Quebec and the Maritime Provinces of Canada, originally settled primarily by emigrants from England and France. The New England states, as one would expect, show the influence of the Mother Country; so does the Tidewater region of Virginia, site of the English settlement of Jamestown as early as 1607. New York State shows a mix of Dutch and English barn styles adapted to the climate and topography of the United States, while the southern Appalachians still have some weath-

ered examples of the sturdy log corn crib-type barns built by early settlers from Sweden and Germany and adopted by other pioneers. This type of construction became increasingly prevalent as settlement moved west to Pennsylvania, Ohio, and what is now the Midwest (originally called the Northwest Territory).

Eventually, almost the entire heavily forested region between the Appalachians and the Mississippi River would be cleared for homesteads and farmed. The principal crops were wheat, corn, oats, and barley, and many families kept a dairy cow, some poultry, a few pigs, and perhaps a yoke of oxen for plowing and hauling. In Canada, settlement spread west through Ontario over a period of several centuries, and the principal crops included wheat,

Opposite: *A classic New England barn trimly painted red and white, the most popular colors for American barns. The two-sloped gambrel roof allows for ample hay storage.*

Left: *A turn-of-the-century photograph from New Brunswick, Canada, shows a peaked-roof barn with a large lean-to on the right, facing a small outbuilding that may have served as a dairy house, chicken coop, or tool shed.*

Above: *Haystacks dot this field on a prosperous New Brunswick farm. The barn has been added onto several times, and the entire farmyard is fenced.*

oats, rye, and buckwheat. What kind of barns housed grain, fodder, and livestock for the Europeans who first settled here and their descendants?

The most common type of early American and Canadian barn was the simple three-bay English barn, originally designed for the storage and threshing of cereal crops, primarily wheat. This barn had a wide side entrance to the threshing floor—the central bay—to admit wagons laden with sheaves. Prior to about 1850, the North American version, which added a second wagon door on the opposite wall, used the two side bays for storing threshed and unthreshed grain, respectively. However, as livestock became more important to the agricultural economy, one of the side bays might be given over to stalls. Alternatively, cattle, sheep, or horses might be housed in an extra bay, or in an L-shaped addition at right angles to the original building.

The hayloft above the threshing floor was used to store fodder. A series of poles with spaces between for ventilation of the hay (to prevent spoilage) was supported on the upper framing of the barn. In larger barns, where the threshing floor was extended into an extra bay, the hayloft was supported by a powerful "swing beam," which might be as long as sixty feet. A North American innovation, the swing beam

took the principal weight of the haymow and also served as part of a sturdy X-shaped truss that helped contain the hay or sheaves. Threshed grain was stored in a bin or room called the granary, which had its prototype in the great European storage barns called granges, where monasteries and manors stored their harvests. In northern Spain, the granary was a small building called the *horreo*, where families or whole villages kept their grain supply. This was a frame structure raised on stone supports at each corner; the supports had flared caps to discourage rats and mice from climbing into the storehouse.

A North American counterpart to the granary is the corn crib, originally made of notched logs. Common in the southern Appalachians, these small structures with gable roofs were often used first as crude dwellings, with the inner walls hewn and chinked with mud or moss. As settlers prospered and built better houses, the log crib was used to store fodder, or to form the nucleus of a full barn. English settlers, influenced by Swedish and German immigrants, built many such barns in Tennessee and the Carolinas. Eventually, a lean-to roof on log supports might be added to one or both sides to shelter wagons and farm implements. By 1875 the Appalachian log barn often housed a crib and a gearshed under a single peaked roof. The slope of these roofs was not so steep as it was farther north, where snow load was a problem. Large expanses of lean-to roofing are rarely seen except where the climate is mild, as in the Deep South and California.

Sometimes large log barns were raised on two sets of cribs with a wagonway running through the middle. The loft was built above the four cribs; usually, it had vertical plank siding and a loft door and winch at one end. Overhung loft barns were built over two cribs, with the roof projecting on all four sides in the form of very broad eaves. Originally, many of these barns had thatched roofs made of such materials as rye straw and salt-marsh reeds. Some had scoop-roofs made of hollowed logs; others were covered with slabs of bark. These roofing materials were eventually replaced by wooden shingles—elm, cedar, or whatever was at hand.

In Georgia, to the early 1800s, log barns were set upon a low stone foundation, and cracks between the logs were covered with narrow slats, or riven clapboards split with a tool called the "froe." It was positioned at the top of the clapoard and struck with a heavy maul to split the wood, then twisted "to and froe" to divide it in half along the full length. Long slats fashioned like shingles were nailed onto the roof from eaves to peak and sometimes chinked with sod or moss. What these modest barns lacked in beauty they made up for in shelter and storage space. As new technology came into use, sawed siding was cut by a multiblade gang saw, and hand-wrought nails were replaced by machine-made products.

Contrary to popular belief, log cabins were not the earliest buildings in Colonial America and Canada: the first permanent European structures were of clapboard on timber framing. Throughout the seventeenth century, this was the dominant building style from Quebec to the southernmost of the original American colonies. The log cabin and barn came to the Atlantic Seaboard in 1638 with the earliest Swedish settlers, along the Delaware River, and was introduced independently by German immigrants after 1700. During the period of westward expansion, the log cabin became increasingly prevalent wherever abundant timber provided the necessary materials, as shown in chapter 4, "Prairie and Western Barns."

Vertical board siding was the most common cladding on early North American barns; horizontal clapboard siding on upright studs was the second most popular form. Sometimes narrow strips of wood called battens were nailed along the spaces between the clapboards to form "board-and-batten" siding. Not only was this more weatherproof, it provided a better appearance as well.

Below: *An isolated farm shows signs of succumbing to the elements, its timbers and planks beginning to give way to the assaults of wind, rain, and frost.*

Above: *A weathered tobacco barn, with full-width doors propped open to dry the crop. Additional ventilation is provided by the wide slits above ground level, which open and close like shutters.*

The barn roofs of New England were more steeply pitched than those of Old England, where a pitch of one-third was the carpenter's norm for shedding water from a thatched roof and minimizing snow load. Curiously, the New England barn roof retained its steep pitch of forty-five degrees or more long after thatch was replaced by shingles, slate, or tile. In Canada, New England Loyalists who emigrated north after the Revolutionary War readopted the British-style barn roof of gentler pitch once the itinerant thatcher passed into history. French-style log construction in Quebec and in northern New England, with its close ties to Canada, is discussed in chapter 3.

Another Colonial barn style that has endured into the present is the Dutch barn, originally built in such areas of Dutch settlement as New York State and New Jersey and widely adopted in other areas, including eastern Canada. The Dutch barn is unmistakable in that the wagon doors are placed at each end of the building rather than "broadside," as in all other North American barns. This plan goes back several

millennia, to European prototypes built with a central nave flanked by aisles (later named the "basilican" plan). Early Christian churches took the same form. So did the medieval "tithe barn," where payments to the church in the form of grain were stored.

In the Netherlands, the basilican form was adapted to the practical requirements of a large threshing floor accessible by wagons and flanked by stalls for livestock. The cattle and horses faced into the central area, from which they were fed, and their winter fodder was stored in a mow above the threshing floor. The stalls were often sunk below the threshing-floor level, as in ancient European barns in which people and livestock were sheltered under one roof in a *Loshoes*, or Long House.

The animals entered and left the barn through a corner door at the gable end of the building. Frequently, this was a two-part "Dutch door," which kept small denizens of the barn inside (or out) while providing light and ventilation through the open upper panel. Over time, many Dutch and English barns were extended by the addition of poultry coops, pig-geries, smokehouses, storage sheds, and other attachments or outbuildings.

Most Dutch Colonial barns were nearly square in plan and had higher eaves than those of the Netherlands, where the eaves were often less than six feet from the ground. The framing of New York State's Dutch barns—centered in the valleys of the Hudson, Schoharie, and Mohawk Rivers—is almost identical with that of their Old World predecessors. The principal difference is that in North America, timbers were almost always sawn, while unsawn trees in their original form, crudely stripped of branches, were often used in Holland. This dates back to the ancient "cruck barn," in which two sets of naturally bent tree trunks were paired to form a cruck, or juncture, at each end of the structure, and braced by a ridgepole. The resulting A-shaped rectangular frame had curved walls filled with a network of interwoven sticks (wattle) covered with mud or plaster. This "wattle-and-daub" type of walling was widely used in Quebec barns of the seventeenth

century, and is occasionally found underlying later forms of siding in old American barns. Another walling technique, called nogging, involved using bricks or plaster to fill in the spaces beween the timber construction posts. Other North American innovations included the use of a gabled and shingled roof, rather than a hipped roof, and sturdy plank threshing floors instead of packed earth.

Eventually, the vernacular architecture of the Atlantic Seaboard was disseminated across the entire continent, with many regional inter-pretations based on indigenous styles, avail-able materials, climate, and new technology. Only a few of North America's original barns have survived to tell their story, described by Canadian historian Eric Arthur as "the story of the master carpenter working with his crew to the point where the great framework of the barn lies ready for a multitude of men, fed and supported on the spot by their womenfolk, who in one long day will put the skeleton structure in position, their only tools being mallets, pike-poles, and levers."

Below: *An unusual New England barn in Wilton, Connecticut, with a front-facing gable above the wagon and hay doors. What appears to be a chimney is a louvered cupola for ventilation.*

Southeastern Barn Styles *Opposite, right, and below*
On the opposite page, sun spills across the old threshing floor
of a timber-frame barn on North Carolina's James River.
Mellowed brick fills the spaces between the windows and
forms decorative arches above them. The small Virginia barn
at right has a steeply peaked roof, with projecting rain hood,
and hay doors at two levels. Below, another Virginia barn
shows the simple, sturdy construction of pioneer carpenters.

Log Construction *Above*
The familiar log cabin, with rough or undressed logs joined
at the corners by notches, seen here on Pelee Island, Ontario.
Pioneer families built such cabins as houses, barns, corn cribs,
and granaries.

Clapboard Siding *Opposite*
West Windsor, Vermont, is the site of this typical New
England barn, with clapboard siding of unequal lengths and a
"tip" or tilted window at the gable end. Most Vermont barns
were painted gray or red and had large cupolas like this one.

Serene Canadian Fields *Above and opposite*
An immaculate farm with shingled buildings (above) looks
to the sea at Springbrook, Prince Edward Island. On the
opposite page, a three-bay English-style barn with board
siding in Milton, Ontario.

Ready for Winter *Above, left*
A well-kept example of rural vernacular architecture in
New York State's Ulster County.

Midwestern Corn Crib *Left*
An in-barn corn crib for fodder storage in Kidron, Ohio.

Past Into Present *Above*
Unbaled hay spills from the mows at Old Sturbridge
Village, in Sturbridge, Massachusetts, an agricultural
museum. On the threshing floor, oxen are yoked for plowing.
The transom above the doors is glazed; originally, such
transoms were covered by a movable board.

Old New England *Right*
A tattered cupola crowns this weather-beaten Connecticut barn, now used for storage. The extension on the left was built for livestock, with a hay door in the gable.

Morrisburg, Ontario *Below*
Historic Canadian barns and other buildings have been preserved at Morrisburg's pioneer and agricultural museum, where patient oxen, dressed for show, play their part in re-creating the past.

Fieldstone Foundations *Below, right*
The Adam Scribner Museum Farm in Weston, Connecticut, has fieldstone foundations characteristic of New England, where pioneer farmers often found that rocks were their most abundant crop. The clapboard-covered house has a pentroof over the small porch, while the barn has vertical board siding.

No Housing Shortage *Right and below*

A handsome colt poses in his Vermont farmyard, while a pair of ducks checks through the straw for something good to eat.

Vermont Dairy Farm *Opposite*

Holsteins graze near the pond in sight of a spacious, bright red dairy barn. Swedish and German immigrants were the first to paint their barns red, with a mixture of red oxide from the soil, linseed from flax, and casein, from cows' milk.

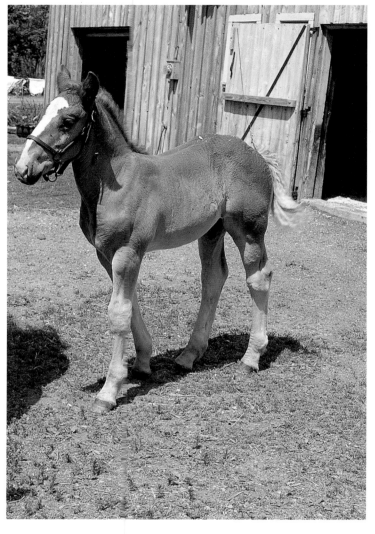

Farmyard Palaces *Right and below*

An unusual number of windows marks the classic New England barn at right (detail opposite) with wagon doors at both ground and upper levels. It is located in Waitsfield, Vermont. The Vermont barn below, in Fayston, has paired and tripled windows on the lower levels and variously shaped openings in the gable.

Representative Roof Styles *Above, right, and opposite*
The rounded roofline on the New England barn above is
the most contemporary of these three examples. Called a
"bow truss roof," it became popular in the early 1900s. To the
right is a gambrel roof with slightly flared eaves and a hooded
hay door—a popular style in the West. The unusual, nearly
flat roof on the opposite page was photographed in New
Brunswick, Canada.

Barns of Prince Edward Island *Opposite and above*
Atlantic Canada has many beautiful and historic barns,
including these photographed at Wheatley (opposite, above),
near Souris (above), and at Burlington (left). Small farms on
the island now face the threat of elimination by incorporation
into larger holdings.

New York State *Right*
Ripening corn forms the foreground for this small barn near Ithaca, with a pentroof over the porch at the gable end. The silos are a later addition.

Substantial New England Barns *Below and opposite*
The barn below, in Quechee, Vermont, has a peaked roof and L-shaped extension. There are numerous windows at the lower (livestock) level and large cupolas on both wings. On the opposite page is a gambrel-roofed barn with paired dormer windows and cupolas.

Peacham, Vermont *Overleaf*
An unusually large barn with three wagon doors, reroofed in metal, forms part of an idyllic New England scene.

The Pennsylvania Style

The handsome two-level banked barn that originated in colonial Pennsylvania was primarily the work of German and Swiss immigrants. Their ethnic building styles were combined and adapted to produce a distinctive vernacular architecture that struck deep roots in their new environment. As historian T. J. Wertenbaker observes in *The Founding of American Civilization: The Middle Colonies:* "We must seek the ancestry of the Pennsylvania-German barn in the wooded highlands of Upper Bavaria, the southern spurs of the Black Forest mountains, in the Jura region and elsewhere in Switzerland." Settlers from these deep valleys and far-ranging hills were accustomed to building their barns (and other structures) into hillsides, with entrances at several levels.

In Upper Bavaria, long house/barns were built at right angles to the slope. They shared a common roof, but the house was a separate, two-story entity at the gable end of the building, while the barn stretched back into the hill. Horses, cattle, and oxen were housed on the lower floor, and the hayloft and threshing floor, made of hewn logs, occupied the upper level. Large boulders were set along the roofline to protect the long roofs from heavy winds.

The Swiss tradition of building with heavy timbers had much in common with the Bavarian. Many of the Swiss were members of the Mennonite sect and had to leave Switzerland in the face of religious persecution. Some sought refuge in the Black Forest region, including ancestors of those who would emigrate to North America during the early 1700s. They shared with the Bavarians a love of color and carving on the house end of their barns and were known as skilled carpenters. In their homeland, they had originally built exclusively in log, later in stone and log, with stabling on the lower level, which was usually sheltered by an overhanging log forebay. Side doors for the animals were at the lower level, while the threshing floor was entered from the hillside, or by a ramp.

Several important changes were made by German and Swiss settlers in the New World. Here, their barns were set parallel to the hillside rather than at a right angle to it. The forebay end of the barn usually faced south, for maximum sunlight and shelter from prevailing winds. The animals were sheltered by the overhang during the winter and shaded during the warmer months. In North America, banked barns were sometimes built entirely of fieldstone: attractive examples survive, not only as working buildings, but as scenic attractions visited and photographed by nostalgic tourists.

Pennsylvania, New York, New Jersey, and Ontario all have two-level barns; most of them are built into a bank so that the drive doors are level with the hilltop. If not, a wide ramp provides access to the second level. The former threshing floor now serves primarily as a storage area for farm implements, with the haymow above and other storage in several bins.

In the German stone barn, the seed room or bin is often a prominent feature, with its own entrance. Hooded doorways for protection from the weather and slit ventilators on stone barns

Opposite: A Pennsylvania dairy barn with ornamental wooden fretwork on the forebay and gable end.

are also characteristic of the Pennsylvania barn. Chimneys on these barns serve as ventilators, carrying away stale air from the stables in their flues rather than smoke from a stove or fireplace. So great is the dread of a barn fire that early colonial law prohibited setting a fire within thirty feet of a barn. Such laws applied even to the blacksmith working at his forge. This fear of fire may be one reason that the combination barn/house building style was not adopted in North America. In the Old World, a peat fire smoldered constantly in the dwelling end of the Long House, but it rarely flared out of control. Log fires offered no such security: their sparks could set off a conflagration that would destroy both livestock and harvest in a single heart-breaking hour.

The Pennsylvania barn was laid out on the basilican plan, like the Dutch barn. The aisles flanking the threshing floor (later called the drive floor) form two galleries. The largest barns of this kind housed many different functions. The stone-walled basement level might provide stalls for half a dozen milk cows and an equal number of horses; root cellars for storing vegetables, fruit, and cider over the winter; feed storage bins; and large loose stalls for cows with calves and for weaning calves. Originally, the upper level was of log construction. By the late nineteenth century, frame construction was the

norm. One of North America's finest log banked barns has been preserved at Black Creek Pioneer Village, an agricultural and folk museum near Toronto, Ontario.

Most of the early banked barns had the over-hanging forebay, or *laube*, of their Swiss and German predecessors. It was supported on heavy timber joists extending from the main floor. This cantilever might project eight to ten feet, sheltering the livestock quarters below. It also provided an area in which to harness horses or oxen, and the enclosed gallery above provided additional storage space. The overhanging bay was a feature of medieval architecture, as seen in the old walled cities of Germany, France, and Britain. Where timbers of sufficient strength to support the forebay were lacking, some protection was offered by the "pentice" or "pentroof"—a canopy projecting only a few feet over the stable wall.

Some of the most impressive Pennsylvania barns are those with gable walls in brick or stone, ornamented with ventilators of various styles. The ventilators may be in the form of narrow slits in the masonry, or patterns formed by omitting bricks at specific intervals—a technique introduced by English settlers. Favorite designs included the "sheaf of wheat," "Gothic window," diamond, starburst, X-shape, and triangle, as illustrated more fully in chapter 5, "Details and Decoration."

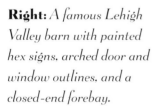

Right: *A famous Lehigh Valley barn with painted hex signs, arched door and window outlines, and a closed-end forebay.*

Left: *Vertical siding defines the clean lines of a German-style barn built near Perrysville, Ohio.*

The brick walls of a Pennsylvania barn, laid up by itinerant bricklayers, were often sixteen inches thick. The bricks were made from local clay on the site, where available, and native limestone was burned in kilns to obtain lime for mortar. Occasionally, one sees a Pennsylvania banked barn made entirely of fieldstone except for the forebay, which, in this case, is a frame extension supported on stone or brick columns. These examples are confined to the southeastern part of Pennsylvania, where many German people settled, including the Amish, originally in Berks and Lancaster Counties.

Like the Shakers, the Amish formed closely knit, hard-working communities whose simple lifestyle and worship were centered in the home. During the early eighteenth century, Amish settlers built small log barns with gabled roofs, like those of other German immigrants. As they prospered, these barns were enlarged, extended, or replaced by buildings with masonry foundations or gable walls. In the process, frame replaced timber as the wooden component of the barn, and the forebay was taken into the main structure by enclosing the open area below it, usually for dairy operations, or to serve as a straw shed. Prior to 1900, straw was often stacked in the open farmyard, where much of it was lost to wind and weather.

According to Stephen Scott, the author of *Amish Houses and Barns*, some conservative Amish still require that all barns be painted red; others leave their barns unpainted, and some communities prefer white barns. Tradition also favors the gabled roof over the roomier gambrel roof. Scott adds that "Among the 'Nebraska' Amish (so called because an early leader had lived in Nebraska) of Mifflin County, Pennsylvania, barn roofs became an issue in a church division. This Amish community had decided that barn roofs were not to have unnecessary projections from the gable ends of the roof. When one member bought a farm from a non-Amish person, and refused to remove these projections from his barn, a heated controversy erupted which eventually ended in a church split in the 1930s. These Nebraska or 'white top' Amish (their buggies have white tops) are among the most conservative Amish anywhere."

Amish farmers have retained some of the outbuildings that became obsolete in the larger society with the advent of electricity. These include the wash house; the summer house, or summer kitchen, for cooking on sultry days; and the spring house, whose cool water still serves as the only source of refrigeration for the most conservative Amish.

Most Amish farms in Lancaster County comprise fewer than 100 acres and are devoted to dairy farming. In recent years, poultry and hog production have also become important. Most of the crops, like corn and hay, are grown to feed the livestock. Large tobacco barns once dotted the county, but some of these have been con-

Right: *Wooden posts help support the forebay, or laube, of this historic Ohio barn, with typical "Dutch" (two-part) doors at the livestock level.*

Right: *Wooden posts help support the forebay, or laube, of this historic Ohio barn, with typical "Dutch" (two-part) doors at the livestock level.*

Below: *An old photograph shows the extent of this Amish farmstead, with several outbuildings, two-story house, and neatly fenced dooryard. Such farms averaged 50–100 acres in size.*

verted to other uses as tobacco farming declined. The former aversion to gambrel roofs has worn away, as most recent barns feature gambrel or hip roofs. Windmills are rapidly being replaced by pneumatic pumps, but wood remains the primary construction material for Amish barns.

The largest Amish community is in Holmes County, Ohio, and dates back to the early nineteenth century. The Yoder-Miller Farm of Holmes County has supported descendants of the Schlabach family for eight generations. Its large wooden banked barn was built about 1840

and has been added to repeatedly. Now it includes a large straw shed, hog house, and silo. Comparable farms still operate successfully in the Elkhart-LaGrange County, Indiana, Amish community.

Historians are still debating the significance of the attractive circular designs known as hex signs painted on many Pennsylvania German barns. Some authorities, including Patricia Mullen, assert that the "hex or witchfoot" was imported from the Rhineland by Mennonite and Amish settlers and used to ward off cow-

fever. Wallace Nutting, writing some fifty years ago, also attributed the hex sign to "a very ancient tradition according to which these decorative marks were potent to protect the barns, or more particularly the cattle, from the influence of witches." Still other historians claim that the hex sign is purely decorative and always was. Contemporary farmers follow the old tradition because the colorful signs are decorative and perhaps, a little, "for luck."

Swiss influence on the banked barn is apparent in the Sweitzer or Switzer barn, built in both single- and double-decker versions. In his book *An Age of Barns*, author and illustrator Eric Sloane calls the Sweitzer barn "the farmyard palace." It began as a simple two-level log structure during the early 1700s and evolved into a larger log barn with a full forebay over a stone stable. By the late eighteenth century, it was a much larger building with stone or brick gable ends, ornamental louvers, patterned brickwork, up to four doors at the lower level, and two or three threshing floors. Horse stables and breeding stalls lined one wall, with oxen and cows in the byre on the opposite wall. Two dry cellars flanked the entrance ramp—one for feed, the other for potatoes— and the central area housed the harness room, straw room, and turnip cellar.

Later German and Dutch farmers used the familiar gambrel roof, sloped at two angles, to make the most of space within the roof area. Some of these were converted from plain peaked roofs and might have a gambrel on only one side and a lean-to on the other. Early roofs had been thatched, where rye straw or marsh reeds were available; others were covered with crude shingles. Cedar was favored as a durable shingle material.

The small doors on most Pennsylvania barns were covered with ornamental hoods, often carved with a heart, a tulip, or a circle giving access to a bird's nest. The large main doors evolved from removable partitions, often without hinges, that were propped shut all winter with a heavy log and removed for the summer. Later, roller doors, adapted from those used for freight cars, came into use. In most cases, a long, glassless "transom light" opening with a hinged shutter was placed above the main door for illumination and ventilation. Eventually, these openings were glazed.

Generations of changes can be read in the stones and timbers of the old Pennsylvania barn. It is easy to see where two, three, and even four additions have been made to the original building; sometimes the masonry shows the scars of enlargement from a narrow single-decker barn to a wider double-decker. Often, the entire farmyard is still enclosed by low stone walls. And the oak framing on complex interior "bents"—vertical posts joined by tie beams and braces—is as strong today as it was for the earliest pioneers.

Below: *An arcade defines the forebay on the German-style barn at the left, viewed from the south.*

Wooden Banked Barns *Left, below, and opposite*
Unusual Gothic louvers (detail at left) grace the venerable banked barn below, in Bedford, Pennsylvania. On the opposite page, a fieldstone foundation supports a weathered barn with silo added. It is still a working building.

Germanic Heritage *Left, below, and opposite*
The rural past is still tangible at Ontario's Mennonite buggy factory (left) in Elmira. Below is Wisconsin's Old World German Farm, with pioneer-style "snake" or zigzag fencing, which eliminated the need to dig post holes. On the opposite page is a Minnesota landmark: the Oliver Kelly Farm, with handsome stone foundation and extensive log fencing.

Banked Barns with Additions *Opposite*
Over time, the barns on the opposite page have been
extended. The modernized Wisconsin barn (opposite, below)
has an open-air corn crib, lightning rods, and several sheds,
while the much-enlarged Ontario barn (opposite, above) has
doubled in size and added several silos.

Lancaster County Amish Barn *Below*
Most Amish barns in the Lancaster, Pennsylvania,
community are painted white and shelter traditional wagons
like this one in White Horse. The original forebay has
been modified.

Holmes County, Ohio, Amish Farms *Right and below*
Corn shocks and stubble recall summer's bounty on the
Amish farm at right in Kidron. On the opposite page (top), a
"driver horse" paces past a double-decker barn with gambrel
roofline. The absence of electrical lines (below), and the
windmill for pumping water, show that this New Hope farm
houses an extended Amish family.

Hex Signs, Lehigh Valley Barns *Opposite and below*
The picturesque Lehigh Valley was settled primarily by
Germans, who modified their traditional building styles to
New World needs but retained distinctive decorative motifs
like the colorful hex signs that beautify these banked barns.
The word "hex" is from the German *Hexe*, a witch, but most
historians and, more importantly, the Pennsylvania farmers
themselves, deny that these signs have any implications of
protection from witchcraft. They are generally considered
purely decorative.

Eastern Ohio *Above*

An unpainted banked barn with off-center gable window overlooks flat, fertile acreage that has been cultivated since the early 1800s, when German settlers from eastern Pennsylvania began to move west.

Durham County, Ontario *Opposite*

A banked barn with wagon drive through the lower level, below the forebay.

Pennsylvania Dairy Barns *Opposite and below*
After the Civil War, dairying became increasingly important,
and many Pennsylvania farms like the one opposite, in
Carpenterstown, were enlarged to meet the demand. The
Lancaster County farm below has both a concrete silo and a
taller wooden silo of twentieth-century vintage.

North of Toledo *Following pages*
Extensions and outbuildings radiate from the original nucleus
of a prosperous farm in rural Ohio.

Connected, Round, and Polygonal Barns

❉ ───────────────────────────────────── ❉

Several unusually shaped barns figure prominently in the history of North American vernacular architecture. The oldest is the connected barn, based on ancient European prototypes touched upon earlier, including the *Loshoes* of the Netherlands and other house/barn combinations designed for the cold climates of central and northern Europe. The round and polygonal forms are indigenous to North America. They evolved during the nineteenth century as a result of new ideas to meet changing conditions in agriculture and animal husbandry and were built sporadically across the continent. Many attractive examples survive, despite the fact that enthusiasm for these unusually shaped barns was of fairly short duration.

French settlers from eastern Canada to the Mississippi Valley brought the age-old tradition of the timber-framed barn/house, called *maison rudimentaire*, from their homeland. The cruck barn, framed in naturally bent timbers that gave it the silhouette of an upturned boat, was in use throughout northern and western France. In Brittany, the *maison bloc* also sheltered people and animals under one roof. From Normandy came the *maison cour*, in which farm buildings were grouped around a central court, either totally enclosed or open at one end to form a U shape. The latter form was the one adapted to North American use. In the *maison cour*, buildings were adjacent to one another but did not share a common roof. However, they are considered here as connected barns, sometimes called "continuous architecture."

In the Low Countries, as mentioned earlier, the connected barn/house was the norm well into the eighteenth century. Frieslanders called the style "head, neck, and body." The compact house formed the head, clearly distinguished by doors, windows, and chimney. The "neck and shoulder" portion served as a churning room or milk cellar, and the barn proper was laid out on the basilican plan. Stalls occupied one side of the central threshing floor, and a wagon passage the other.

Connected log barns were built in Scandinavia and imported to North America by Swedish, Norwegian, and Danish immigrants. The Swedes came first, to settle along the Delaware River; later immigrants moved progressively farther west and concentrated in the upper Midwest, whose lakes and streams were reminiscent of their homeland. Scandinavian barns included those built of two boxlike pens, or cribs, of log with an open passage between. A continuous sod roof united the two structures—and provided a convenient grazing place for the family goats, who might otherwise stray into trouble, in the manner of goats everywhere. One of the cribs served for grain or hay storage and the other as a byre. This design was a forerunner of the so-called dogtrot barns of the southern Appalachians and the regions west of the mountains. The dogtrot would recur in the ranch house and livestock shelters of cattle country after 1850.

The two-story log barn of galleried form was characteristic of northern Sweden. A sill of hewed logs rested on padstones placed under

Opposite: *A trim polygonal barn in Waitsfield, Vermont, with a hip roof and central cupola. The polygonal form was easier to engineer and build than the round barn, which posed problems in fitting siding, windows, and doors.*

Above and below:

Examples of continuous farms and architecture in eastern Canada, where severe winters dictated closely connected quarters.

key sections of the walls. A single-story lean-to was often built at one or both ends, and a pent-roof sheltered the wagon doors. In Norway, squared and notched timbers were used to construct two-story barns much like those of Germany. A cantilevered upper story held the haymow, with stalls and fodder storage areas at the basement level. Outbuildings were often connected to the main barn for protection from severe winters. All of these forms would be adapted to local conditions in the New World.

Fortunately, the earliest history of connected barns in North America has been preserved in the archives of the Province of Quebec, which date back to the sixteenth century. More detailed information survives in seventeenth-century records, as discussed by Canadian historians Eric Arthur and Dudley Witney in *The Barn: A Vanishing Landmark in North America*. They report that the first Canadian farmer was Louis Hèbert, who grew grain and vegetables near Quebec beginning in 1615; they surmise that Monsieur Hèbert and his family "must have farmed entirely by the labour of their hands and the sturdiness of their backs, for it was not until 1628 that a son-in-law in France sent them a wooden plough. They waited until 1647 for their first sight of a horse...."

Several Jesuit missions in Canada made early contributions to New World agriculture, including the mission of Ste. Marie to the Hurons, founded in 1639 near present-day Midland, Ontario. Destroyed by the Hurons ten years later with total loss of life, this outpost of the "Black Robes," as they were called, had a two-level log barn of rugged palisade construction that has been faithfully rebuilt using the methods of seventeenth-century France. Narrow windows flank the crude doors to the stable area, which is protected by a modest overhang that served as protection against snow sliding off the roof—a matter of some concern in an area where winter snowfall can amount to 150 inches. Before they were killed by the Hurons, founders Jean de Brebeuf and Gabriel Lalement had succeeded in harvesting cereal crops including barley and oats, as well as native corn and sunflowers.

Another kind of connected barn is found principally in New England and eastern Canada. Known as the New England barn, it is a series of units grouped in either a straight line or an ell, usually with an irregular roofline. A variation on the basic English barn, it may be enlarged by bays to form additional drive floors, mows, or stabling. Sometimes the complex includes only house, woodshed, and barn; more often, it takes in several other structures—sheep pen, dairy house, piggery, hen house, tool shed, or additional hay storage sheds. Almost all these

barns are of clapboard construction, although shingle siding is sometimes found in eastern New England. Cedar and birch logs, some still clad in bark, support the main structures.

In *American Barns and Covered Bridges*, Eric Sloane suggests that "the early barn is the best example of American colonial architecture....The barns in Europe were small, just big enough to house a few horses or cattle, but when [settlers] built an American barn, it became the symbol of a new life. From the beginning, the American barn was big, like the hopes and plans for life in the New World."

An English visitor to New England wrote home in 1800 that: "The farms are like little attached villages." Prevailing winds and weather dictated both the form of the connected barn and its placement on the site—"well into the weather." Saltbox barns, with a long, low roofline facing north, were banked on that side with straw, sod, and cornhusks for insulation. Early weather vanes, usually made of wood, helped

Below: *Smokehouses for fish and a barn for crop storage raised above the high-water mark in the seaside community of Seal Cove on Grand Manon Island, New Brunswick.*

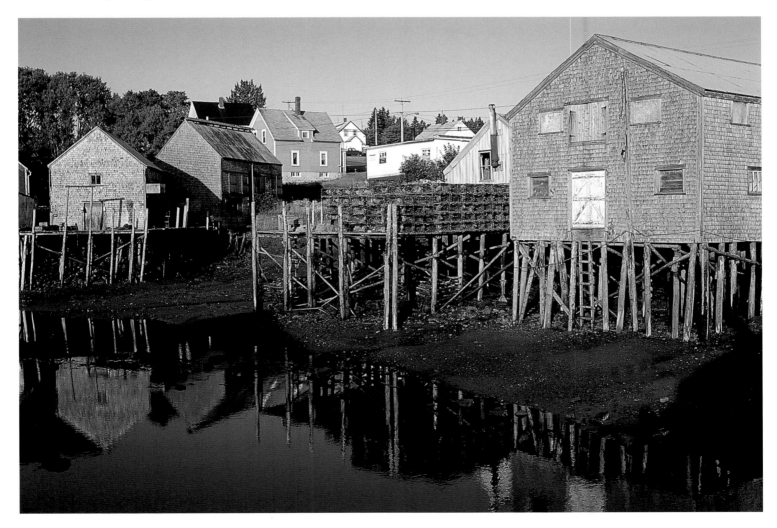

Right: *An 1885 photograph of the round stone dairy barn built by the Shaker community at Hancock, Massachusetts, and imitated widely by progressive farmers.*

the farmer plan his tasks for the day and keep the entries in his weather almanac.

Over time, many farmers closed off the door between house and barn, or moved the house bodily to adjacent ground. Even then, continuous fences connected house and farmyard, for it was not unknown for a farmer to lose his bearings in a blizzard and freeze to death within yards of shelter. Fences and even ropes provided guidelines to safety.

The round barn and its cousin, the polygonal barn, were experiments during the early 1800s and achieved some popularity before the turn of the century. These unusual and attractive barns would eventually be built in all agricultural regions, but they never achieved the acceptance of traditional forms, and many have passed from use. They posed new problems in framing, siding, and stabling. The basic idea was sound: the circle does enclose maximum interior space with minimal walling. It also provides convenience in feeding cattle from a central mow — sometimes with an interior silo — ringed by stalls facing into the mow. However, as Eric Sloane points out, "hay storage required complicated devices for loading, and the pie-shaped stalls would have been best only for pie-shaped animals."

The set-up for these unusual barns was more demanding than that for the familiar rectangular form, and a single mistake in engineering could compromise the entire structure. However, progressive farmers of the later 1800s found much to admire in the round barn built by a Shaker community in Hancock, Massachusetts, in 1865 on stone foundations laid for an earlier barn in 1824. This handsome feat of engineering by Shaker masons and carpenters inspired imitators across the continent into the twentieth century. It was hailed by influential farm journals as "a model for the soundest dairying practice" at a time when large-scale dairy farming was coming into its own due to urban and suburban growth.

Now a museum, this great barn is ninety feet in diameter and two stories high. It is built of stone and crowned by a clerestory (a band of windows below the roofline) and a cupola. The mow measures fifty-five feet across and is separated from the wide feeding aisle and the stalls by a low parapet. Timbers form an octagonal column in the center that supports the superstructure. Most round barns were on a smaller scale and were built of timber, although stone barns are seen on the Canadian plains.

Octagonal and other multisided barns had few precedents. Progressive "gentleman farmers" like George Washington had experimented with the form. Washington built a sixteen-sided structure on one of his Fairfax County, Virginia, properties in 1793. And Thomas Jefferson introduced an octagonal summer house in nearby Bedford County thirteen years later. But it was not until the early 1840s that the octagonal form was popularized, by phrenologist Orson S. Fowler. In his book *A Home for All, or the Gravel Wall and Octagon Mode of Building*, Fowler made an enthusiastic case for the healthfulness and convenience of octagonal houses. In 1853 he extended his zeal to the farmyard, asserting that "In [barns] especially we need some common *center* in and around which to work. This form will turn heads of all the horses and cattle and openings to all the bays and bins toward the center," providing for economy of movement. By the 1880s, hundreds of octagonal barns had been built from plans published in agricultural journals.

A later example, in Michigan's Tuscola County, dates from the early 1920s. Banker James Purdy built a huge octagonal timber-framed barn to house a herd of Black Angus cattle. Almost 100 feet in diameter, the Purdy barn has walls 48 feet high under a 2-stage roof pierced by shed dormers projecting from the clerestory. As in the Shaker barn at Hancock, an unusual number of windows provides the interior with ample light. Feed was dropped from the mow to the central floor space, and an overhead tramway loaded and unloaded hay from the main loft. By this time, mechanization was increasingly replacing many of the laborious chores of the past.

The second half of the nineteenth century brought new unity to the North American continent. Railroads had connected the coasts, and a new generation of pioneers was putting down roots in the Far West. The distinctive barns that evolved to meet changing times and conditions are described in the following chapter.

Below: *A round barn built in Michigan's Big Rapids area in the late 1800s has been much enlarged during the present century.*

Country Road *Above*
A shingled barn enlarged by a lean-to holds its own beside a
weathered hay barn falling into disrepair.

Agricultural and Pioneer Museums *Opposite*
These historical sites featuring examples of preserved
connected barns include, from top, Upper Canada Village,
Ontario; the Van Allen House, New York State; and Old
Fort William, Thunder Bay, Ontario.

Connected Additions *Below, right, and opposite*
The connected barn below, in North Branford, Connecticut, is typical of the post-pioneer era; additions were built as the farm outgrew the original central building. A small dormer breaks the roofline of the middle section. The winter scene at right features an extended farmstead in East Montpelier, Vermont. Many northern New England barns were built adjoining the family home by French settlers during the Colonial era; those that were preserved have been further extended over time. Square cupolas, like the two shown here, are among the features that usually help to identify the older parts of the farmstead. The original central barn from St. Jacobs, Ontario (opposite, below), is flanked by two additions and a single silo.

Angles and Planes *Opposite and above*
The connected barns on the opposite page are from the
American Midwest; both have been progressively extended to
accommodate the increasing storage needs of the farms. The
example above, a cluster of barn buildings, is in Ontario's
Ottawa Valley. In this photograph, the severe geometry of the
bright red barns is softened by the rolled hay bales.

Evolution of a Working Building *Above and left*
It is difficult to date old barns, because so many farms "just grew" like Topsy, incorporating elements of the past with new features like conical silos and hay-handling equipment. Both the historic barns above are in Vermont, one in sight of a modern ski resort. The Midwestern complex at left charts decades of growth in the form of additions, extensions, and modernization.

Peaked and Rounded Rooflines *Above*

The large cupola on the peaked roof of this Fletcher,
Vermont, dairy farm denotes the original nineteenth-
century building. The gently sloping and rounded roofs
cover later additions.

An Eclectic Combination *Right*

This imposing barn with its own windmill began with
the gambrel-roofed building on the right, raised on a
fieldstone foundation. Enlarged repeatedly, it commands
a view of extensive acreage under cultivation in
southwestern Wisconsin.

Hancock Shaker Village, Massachusetts

Above and opposite

A landmark in North American agriculture, the round stone barn first built by the Shakers of Hancock, Massachusetts, in 1826 has been preserved as a working farm that is part of a museum. Its walls are almost a yard wide, and it housed fifty-two head of cattle, with an immense hay-storage capacity in the central mow, from which they were fed.

Turn-of-the-Century Round Barns *Above and opposite*
The enthusiasm for round barns soon spread from New
England to other parts of the continent. Many were built in
Vermont, including the one above in West Barnet. They were
also popular on the plains of Saskatchewan, where the two on
the opposite page, with interior silos, were photographed.
Round barns were commonly built of wood, stone, or a
combination of both.

Interrupted Rooflines *Opposite*

At top is the McFarlane round barn, southwest of Glen Ewen, Saskatchewan. Continuous windows at the livestock level light the interior, and the huge hay door has a peaked rain hood. Below is the polygonal Brown pig barn, southeast of Harris, Saskatchewan, lighted entirely by windows in the cupola.

Polygonal Cattle Barn *Above*

This elaborate polygonal barn with two-stage roof was built in Tuscola County, Michigan, to house a herd of Black Angus cattle. Almost 100 feet in diameter, it has walls 48 feet high. Shed dormers project from the clerestory in this unusual design.

Classic Round Barns *Opposite, above, and right*

The elegant barn on the opposite page, with bell-shaped cupola and painted horses, is south of Traverse City, Michigan. To the right is another handsome Midwestern barn, with an unusual convex roofline and windows at three levels. Clerestory windows high in the walls illuminate the barn above, in Irasburg, Vermont.

New England Polygonal Barns *Opposite and above*
The pleasing symmetry of the historic polygonal barn at
Waitsfield, Vermont (above), has made it a local landmark.
On the opposite page is the unique Bradley-Wheeler
Barn, built about 1850 and preserved by the Westport,
Connecticut, Historical Society. This seven-sided building
of cobblestone and brick construction (detail above) is the
work of a master mason.

Prairie and
Western Barns

✳ ——————————————————————————— ✳

The nineteenth century brought profound changes to North American agriculture, as the population moved steadily westward and new tools and technology became available. German, Scotch-Irish, and Scandinavian settlers from the Middle Atlantic and Appalachian regions staked major claims in the Midwest, taking their traditional methods of barn-building with them. Many people of French descent occupied the Mississippi Valley as far south as New Orleans, where the great river enters the Gulf of Mexico. There was considerable movement across the Canadian border, as some Canadians moved south into Michigan and surrounding areas and a number of Americans emigrated to Canada.

Thus the Pennsylvania, New England, and French *"pièce sur pièce"* log barn occurred over a wider-than-ever geographical area. The latter style featured upright logs set between a wooden sill and an overhead plate, and fastened at the corners. It was especially prevalent in Canada and the Midwest. However, when the migrating farmer reached the Great Plains and the Far West, he had to rethink his whole approach to sheltering his family, crops, and livestock.

For one thing, wood was scarce on the Great Plains, and water was not always at hand. High winds swept over the grasslands, bringing fierce storms in both summer and winter. The dry climate loosened traditional timber fastenings like the wooden trunnel, or peg, and the mortise joint.

Opposite: *An old prairie barn near Mankota, Saskatchewan, with sheds attached for livestock and implements.*

Left: *Settlers of Saskatchewan raise a saltbox prairie barn at the turn of the century.*

Above: *Canada's pre-eminent "big barn": the W.T. Smith Ranch barn in Leader, Saskatchewan. It measured 128 feet wide and 400 feet long, with 875,000 board feet of lumber used in construction.*

Where wooden roof shingles had expanded in a damp climate like that of the Connecticut River Valley, keeping the barn watertight, they were far likelier to shrink and blow away on the prairie. And even where wood was plentiful, there was no time to let it season—or dry properly—for up to a year, as in "the old days" of the colonial era.

The Western pioneer often improvised livestock shelters from pole frameworks covered with hay or straw before a proper barn could be constructed. In *American Barns and Bridges*, Eric Sloane quotes a mid–nineteenth-century book entitled *Barn Plans and Outbuildings* that describes the advantages of such ready-made shelters:

> *Farmers in the newer portions of the West do not have stables for their cattle or snug sheds for their sheep. Stock raisers are called upon to make the winter as comfortable as possible for their animals with the limited means at their command. Sheds of poles with roofs of straw are extensively used and with profit. They furnish at the same time shelter from storms and feed for the protected animals. New hay is packed on after each storm. Those who have traveled over the cattle ranges of the West have been struck with the skill displayed in the construction of these shelters.*

Several Western barn styles became prominent during the 1800s, which would become the age of "big barns." One version had a two-story hay-storage center with open peaks for ventilation, protected by projecting rain hoods. It was flanked by large single-story lean-tos for the livestock. Hay was loaded mechanically into doors high in the gable ends. Another style featured a huge gambrel roof with low side walls, designed to deflect the wind, with wagon doors on one side and hay doors in the gables. The prairie corn barn was a single-story wooden structure with a wagon door at one or both ends. It contained large storage bins and a threshing floor. An attached lean-to provided wagon and implement storage.

Although traditional Eastern hardwoods were in scarce supply, sawed softwoods precut to standard dimensions were widely available from sawmills, and new construction methods evolved to meet prevailing conditions. By the end of the century, timber framing had been largely replaced by two new building methods. In stick-frame construction, light walls supported on upright studs, and roofs carried on board frameworks called trusses, took the place of heavy post-and-beam sections pegged together. The second technique, called balloon framing, formed the framework from small members nailed together. The studs extended the full height of the building—usually two stories—in contrast to platform framing, in which each floor was framed separately.

Cattle ranchers often used a kind of glorified haystack called the field barn to shelter their stock. The haystack, covered by a conical roof, was raised on fencelike stanchions through which the cattle fed. According to Eric Sloane, *Farm Quarterly* endorsed this method as recently as 1954, when it published an article that asked: "Do we need any barns for beef cattle? The field barn that is built right where the hay is cut, and cattle fed through stanchions below it, makes an ideal wind shelter and automatic feeding station."

Another nineteenth-century innovation was the upright silo, which replaced the traditional trench silo for storing fodder. According to Eric Arthur and Dudley Witney, "An article dated 1885 states that the system of storing green fodder is of Hungarian origin, introduced in 1875 to British farmers in an article in the *Journal* of the Royal Agricultural Society. At that time, the system consisted of cramming the green fodder tightly into deep wide trenches—wetness having the merit, it was claimed, of easy packing and of preservation." Sometimes the silage was simply stacked on the ground in a long, low pile and covered with ground limestone and sawdust, as in the trench method. In either case, spoilage was minimal.

Apparently, it was an Illinois farmer named Fred Hatch who built the first upright silo, during the 1870s. Soon these picturesque structures were springing up like mushrooms all over North America. They were built of brick and stone, as well as wood, in both circular and square forms. In Western round barns, they were sometimes enclosed within the structure, as mentioned in the previous chapter. The commonest form of silo was a cylinder of thin boards bound by wire hoops, put up beside the barn. Often, it leaned at an angle dictated by prevailing winds or by the most recent storm.

The most popular form of silage was corn, which was highly nutritious and increased the milk yield of dairy cows. The entire corn plant was chopped to pieces by a feed cutter and blown through a pipe into the top of the silo, where it was occasionally trodden down to expel air. Although it originated in the Midwest, the silo was eagerly accepted by Eastern farmers with growing dairy operations. Some half a million silos had been constructed by the early 1900s.

Several familiar outbuildings were modified over time, including the corn crib, which the first settlers had placed underground, as the Native Americans did. Later cribs were built of notched logs, sometimes with a wagon drive between them. Finally, the corn crib evolved into a small structure with slatted walls slanting outward to the eaves. This permitted air to pass around the corncobs, drying them for storage and preventing mold. These sheds were usually

Left: *A tattered wooden barn gives way to the elements on an abandoned Michigan farm.*

Right: *A sturdy silo of multicolored fieldstone, painstakingly constructed on a farm near Charlevoix, Michigan, to last for more than a lifetime.*

raised on posts topped by pie tins or glass to prevent rodents from entering. Sometimes there were two cribs, one for soft corn, the other for hard, or seasoned, corn.

During the 1800s, metal hardware for barn hinges and fittings became widely available. Originally, barn hinges were made of hardwoods like rock maple, sometimes secured by iron staples, or of thick leather attached by hand-wrought nails. Both wooden and metal pegs used for joinery were nicked to increase their holding power before they were hammered into place — a practice Eric Sloane relates to our expression "fitting a round peg into a square hole." Even as the iron foundries were depleting North American forests for fuel, Western farmers were becoming increasingly dependent on metal hardware. Traditional carpentry skills were on the wane in the face of new technology.

Another feature of the prairie and Western barn was the windmill, used primarily to pump water. Early versions took several forms, including one with a movable pole on a wagon wheel and another equipped with a vane for automatic direction. The wind pump with annular sails

(arranged in a circle) was introduced by American inventor Daniel Hallady in 1854 and adapted to production in steel by Stuart Perry some thirty years later. Eventually, it came into worldwide use as a cheap and reliable source of power.

Other innovations fostered by farm journals and supply catalogues included the manure trolley, a mechanical device that replaced the cumbersome wheelbarrow in transporting odorous but effective fertilizer from stall to field, and the sliding barn door, which soon became the norm. Ventilation grew more sophisticated, with wind-driven rooftop rotors drawing air through ducts placed all over the barn. This not only provided more hygienic conditions for livestock, but decreased the chance of spontaneous combustion in the haymow. Mechanical hay carriers, elaborate cupolas and weather vanes, lightning rods, and flexible stanchions were some of the products that had their day in the sun.

By 1900 the face of rural North America had changed in many irreversible ways. The demographic shift from country to city took its toll on the traditional family farm. New immigrants, too, were settling in the larger cities to become

factory workers rather than homesteaders. Land holdings grew larger and were cultivated more intensively to meet the needs of burgeoning urban populations. Specialization became the norm, as cattle and sheep ranchers focused on crops like corn and alfalfa for livestock feed; tobacco growing, once widely practiced as a lucrative sideline, was concentrated in a few regions; and cereal crops like wheat flowed across vast areas of the Prairie states. Over time, many old barns were abandoned, to sink back into the earth under the onslaught of wind and weather. Fields that had known the heavy tread of oxen and draft horses, the clatter of wagons and threshing machines, the rustle of cornstalks and the whirring of wings, as birds came to garner their share of the harvest, lay fallow and untended. Fortunately, however, many beautiful old barns have been preserved, repaired, or converted to new uses, thus guaranteeing a visible link to our irreplaceable rural heritage.

Left: *A venerable Wisconsin barn with ornamental windows high in the gable end.*

Below: *An old log barn is the foundation for a refurbished, gambrel-roofed shelter in Cypress Hills, Saskatchewan.*

Midwestern and Alberta Board Barns

Above and opposite

Saw mills provided the raw material for these nineteenth-
century barns. The one above has been enlarged by a roomy
lean-to. On the opposite page (top), extended eaves supported
on wooden posts form a storage porch at Minnesota's
Lumbertown, USA. The fenced farmyard below, with
inquisitive goose, is in Seebe, Alberta.

Shingled Barn *Above*
Now falling into disrepair, this shingled barn on a fieldstone foundation was the pride of a Midwestern farmer in its day.

Windmills as Landmarks *Opposite*
Towering windmills mark the sites of Heritage Hill (top), a time-honored Belgian farm in Green Bay, Wisconsin, and a picturesque Michigan homestead silhouetted by winter sunlight.

Grain and Corn Barns *Opposite and below*
The cultivation of cereal crops like wheat, alfalfa, and corn
helped shape Western barns like the Idaho storage barn
opposite and the nearly windowless prairie barn below, with
its twin silos.

Midwestern Storage Barns *Opposite and below*
Both of these barns are typical of the Cornbelt and reflect the
axiom found in a well-worn copy of the *Carpenter's Pocket
Dictionary*: "Strength and convenience are the two most
essential requirements in building; the due proportion and
correspondence of parts constituting a beauty that always first
attracts the eye; and where that beauty is wanting, carving
and gilding only excite disgust."

Early Twentieth Century *Opposite and above*
Twin metal cupolas (detail opposite, above) serve as "date
stones" on the symmetrical prairie barn above, which has an
unusual number of windows above and below. It was
photographed in Zealandia, Saskatchewan. The barn
opposite, below, framed by cattails, borders a Michigan pond.

California Barns *Above and below*
Typical of Western stock farms are these well-ventilated barns
that serve as fodder storage and feeding centers in the mild
climate of the Southwest.

Progressive Farming, Wisconsin *Below*
This unusual boat-shaped barn with metal roof, raised on a
concrete-block foundation, soon became a landmark near Eau
Claire, where dairy farming flourishes to this day.

Pioneer Log Barns *Above and opposite, below*
Generations of westward migration are recorded in the
failing timbers of these once-weathertight prairie barns.

Fair Share *Opposite, above*
Rich Midwestern fields attract an eager flock in search of
good things turned up by the plow. A spacious gambrel-
roofed barn presides over the scene.

Gateway to the West *Above*

Many settlers found the hilly, wooded countryside of
Missouri so congenial that they looked no farther and built
homesteads there. This central Missouri barn has stood for
more than a hundred years.

Wide Open Spaces *Below*
Echo Valley Farm in Saskatchewan houses crops and
livestock in this well-built prairie barn with a single cupola
and a large hay door sheltered by a rain hood.

Historic Wooden Barns *Opposite and above*
Multipaned windows illuminate the ground-level stalls
of the Midwestern barn on the opposite page, built into a
hillside in the German style. The ell-shaped barn above,
with its gleaming roof and silo, commands acres of Great
Plains farmland. Both buildings have been refurbished
over the years.

New England Antecedents *Above and left*
Tilt windows, white trim, and peaked gables announce the
ancestry of Domino Farm (above) in Ann Arbor, Michigan,
and the immaculate Wisconsin barn at left.

Midwestern Pastoral *Opposite*
White horses share pastures near a beautiful Claire,
Michigan, dairy barn with bow truss roofline and twin silos.

Canadian Storage Barns *Opposite and below*
Grain and hay storage are pre-eminent features of these beautifully kept barns. The one on the opposite page, in Austin, Manitoba, has a capacious bow-truss roof, as does the barn at the foot of this page, in Annapolis Valley, Nova Scotia. The gambrel-roofed barn below, rising from a flowering orchard, is on the Bay of Quinte, Ontario.

From the Heartland *Opposite and below*
On the opposite page, acres of pumpkins proclaim a
banner year for a mellow Midwestern farm complex.
In the photograph below, rhythmically alternating circles,
squares, and octagons comprise a pattern of rare beauty
near Salinas, Michigan.

Details and Decoration

Originally, North American barns were almost devoid of ornamentation. They were raised to serve the essential purpose of shelter in small clearings hacked from the forest. Sometimes the bark was left on the logs or timbers, and clapboard siding was unpainted. Over time, however, as farmers prospered and different ethnic strands were woven together into a vernacular architecture, the humble barn took on new color and light, as paint and whitewash, windows, louvers, and cupolas became ornamental as well as useful.

Swiss and German immigrants were used to painting their barns in bright primary colors—blues, reds, and yellows—that emphasized exposed beams, joists, and rafter ends. The house end of the European connected barn usually had decorative painting and carving as well. In the New World, both time and materials for such ornamentation were in short supply. Farmers from central Europe began to paint their barns red or red and white, mainly to protect the weatherboards, but also to preserve tradition. Some authorities believe that the white outlines around American barn doors and windows were originally used to protect the structure from evil forces; others call this a ridiculous idea, while they also dispute the belief that hex signs were meant to ward off witchcraft. Less controversial, and very popular, were patriotic themes: portraits of George Washington, the Stars and Stripes, "1776."

Some farmers painted or carved quotations from the Scriptures on their barns, like "Teach me thy way, O Lord." This was especially common, although not limited to, devout members of sects like the Mennonites and Amish. Forthright reminders like "Get right wih God" and "Jesus Saves" are still commonly seen, especially in the South. Carving, as such, is seldom found, although the keystones of segmental arches on a stone barn might be carved with a sheaf of wheat or an evergreen, both being ancient symbols of fertility and new life. Sometimes the mason's mark is found inside the barn along with the farmer's initials.

Carved datestones are a real find for students of vernacular architecture. Not long ago, an incised stone lintel dating from 1863 was discovered near Guelph, Ontario. Flanked by four-pointed stars in circles, the inscription reads:

Opposite: *A Renaissance portrait by Doug Tyler, after Piero della Francesca's Federico da Montefeltro, raises this Michigan barn to new levels of artistry.*

Below: *A whimsically crafted mailbox greets visitors to this Pennsylvania farm.*

Above: *Roof and silo merge gracefully on a barn at the Children's Museum in Dartmouth, Bristol County, Massachusetts.*

"When your barn is well filled, all snug and secure, Be thankful to God and remember the poor." In the old barns of Quebec, a statue of Christ was sometimes placed in a niche over the door, just as the cross appears on the Spanish granaries of Galicia.

Pennsylvania barns are famous for their circular hex signs enclosing traditional designs like the star, heart, whirling swastika, tulip, and other flower forms. Barn decoration reached the level of folk art in this state and other areas settled by Swiss and German immigrants, as seen in chapter 2. Paintings of livestock also abound in Pennsylvania, usually rendered as simple sil-

houettes of the dairy cow, draft horse, or other animal for which the farm is known. In eastern Canada, paintings of sturdy horses like the French-bred Percheron and the English Clydesdale were especially popular. Rarely seen today, but very attractive, is wooden fretwork in geometric patterns, inset as panels or applied as bargeboards to frame a gable, like the "gingerbread" trim on Victorian houses.

Similar to Pennsylvania in beauty and vitality are the barns of Quebec. Here it is the wagon doors that are painted in brilliant colors and designs that suggest professional artistry. In fact, it was almost always the farmer or his wife who created these welcome bursts of color in the landscape. In the French tradition, many Quebec barns were whitewashed. A mixture of lime and water, often combined with a pure grade of ground chalk called whiting, was first used in Canada more than 300 years ago.

Even the fine arts have found their way onto barns, as seen in the following plates. Larger-than-life copies of masterworks by Renaissance masters like Leonardo da Vinci and Hans Holbein have been displayed. At the opposite extreme are the many examples of billboard-style advertising: "Chew Bull Durham" and "Mail Pouch Tobacco: Treat Yourself to the Best." These were usually applied by zealous traveling salesmen who made their rounds with offers to paint the barn if they could feature their message. Less frequent, but striking, are original works of art by talented local painters—galloping horses, stylized landscapes, family portraits, and colorful montages.

Masterful stone- and brickwork are especially characteristic of the Pennsylvania barn, wherever it is found, and of conservative sects who built for the ages, including the Mennonites and the Shakers. The careful placement of native stones and locally made bricks in their courses is a study in pattern and texture. So are the handsome designs created by the omission of a number of bricks or stones for ventilation purposes. Wooden barns, too, have their ornamental louvers, shutters, and pigeonholes under the eaves or over the doors. These holes were left to provide access and nesting sites for swallows and martins, which consumed insects, and for the pigeons that often turned up in pies. Sometimes an ornamental dovecote or martin house is found nearby in the farmyard.

Fencing is another feature that varies widely from one region to another. The pioneers used any material available, ranging from tree roots (also used for crude livestock shelters) to split rails and zigzag "snake" fences. Fieldstone fencing laid up without mortar, called drywall, is typical of New England, where ancient glaciers left an inexhaustible supply of stones that had to be removed from the fields before cultivation. In Virginia and Kentucky horse country, well-finished wooden fencing encloses many acres of pastureland.

Weather vanes appeared on North American barns during the early days of settlement and became more ornate and sophisticated during the nineteenth century. The first weather vanes were carved from wood or forged in blacksmiths' shops and special forge barns—tool houses and "repair shops" where farmers mended their own implements and created new tools. These barns were never used for livestock or grain storage, as a fire burned in them year round. Sometimes they sheltered the family before a proper farmhouse could be built: thus the few remaining examples have chimneys, doors, and windows resembling those of a small house.

Early weather vanes took the form of arrows, pointing hands, horses, and roosters—the latter accounts for the word "weathercock." As ani-

Below: *Virginia Thoroughbreds graze in their roomy enclosures in "horse country," where the importation of the English horse Bule Rock, a son of the Darley Arabian, in 1830, became the foundation of Thoroughbred breeding in the United States.*

Right: *A running horse spins above the cupola of a gray barn in Wilton, Connecticut.*

Rooftop ventilators in the form of cupolas originated in the Connecticut Valley and were widely adopted elsewhere. Each farmer designed his own, usually in the form of a square or rectangular turret with louvers or windows on all four sides and a gabled or hipped roof topped by a weather vane. Sometimes the cupola had pigeonholes or carved designs and appeared in pairs or triplets along the roofline. It was also used on ice houses, spring houses, and apple-drying barns. Occasionally, a very large cupola that served as an observatory, reached by a stairway, was built on a wealthy farm, or designed by an architect. A rare example, later destroyed with the barn in a windstorm, was the room-size cupola on the Jackson estate at Mount Rose, New Jersey. A Shaker barn in New York State has a cupola the size of a two-story cottage!

mal husbandry became more widespread, cows and pigs became popular figures on the rooftop or cupola. During the later decades of the nineteenth century, both weather vanes and cupolas of elaborate design could be ordered from farm-supply catalogues. Horses and cows were most in demand, but farmers in seaside communities might display a fish or a whale.

Old tobacco barns survive in a variety of interesting designs based on their function as drying barns. Some have hinged vertical vent boards painted to contrast with the rest of the siding. This type is indigenous to Kentucky; most Southern tobacco barns were not painted. Maryland farmers built hip-roofed barns with hinged panels that swung outward, both

Below: *A row of elegant square cupolas provide ventilation for the large barn whose roof they adorn.*

Left: *Safe, accessible tool storage was often accommodated by sturdy hooks or rings mounted on an interior wall.*

Below: *An old hay cutter, harrow, and draft-team "tractor" retired to a field of wildflowers—antique Americana.*

vertically and horizontally. Hinged siding was also used on Connecticut tobacco barns, which were either unpainted or painted red and white. The "top hat" tobacco barn had open gables shielded by projecting rain hoods and window-size vents to increase air flow to the leaves, which hung from closely spaced poles. On small farms, tobacco leaves were often simply nailed to the roof boards of the hay barn for curing.

Handmade tools and implements, rarely considered objects of beauty by their creators, now form handsome features of farm- and pioneer-museum collections in the United States and Canada. They include the broad axe, used for hewing and squaring logs; augers for drilling holes in timber; chisels and mallets; and story poles with incised measurements, used to lay out barn framing. Carpenters' marks were cut into the timbers to indicate their placement in the prefabricated framework. Other objects of homely beauty, now become increasingly rare, are wagon and buggy frames, great wooden snow rollers, and the scythes, flails, and winnowing trays used to harvest grain until the advent of the first threshing machines. Each of these time-worn objects has its own story to tell. The photographs on the following pages illustrate the ingenuity and artistry of countless farming families who made their barns as beautiful as they were functional.

Hex Signs *Opposite and below*
Traditional designs including the whirling swastika, the star,
and flower forms on these Pennsylvania and Ohio barns carry
on a tradition that began with the immigration of Germans
from the Rhineland and Bavaria, where hearts are also
popular motifs.

The Brick Barn *Below*

Yellow and clay-colored bricks form a pleasing façade on this modernized Dutch-style barn in Berlin, Ohio. Where suitable clay was available, pioneer masons made bricks on site. Today, they come from the factory.

Gable Ornaments *Opposite*

A high-stepping show horse graces the gable of the Strasburg, Pennsylvania, barn at the top of the opposite page. Below it, Gothic louvers and a five-pointed star appear on a wooden barn in Highspire, Pennsylvania. Such decorative features can fulfill a fuction, often ventilation, while others are purely decorative.

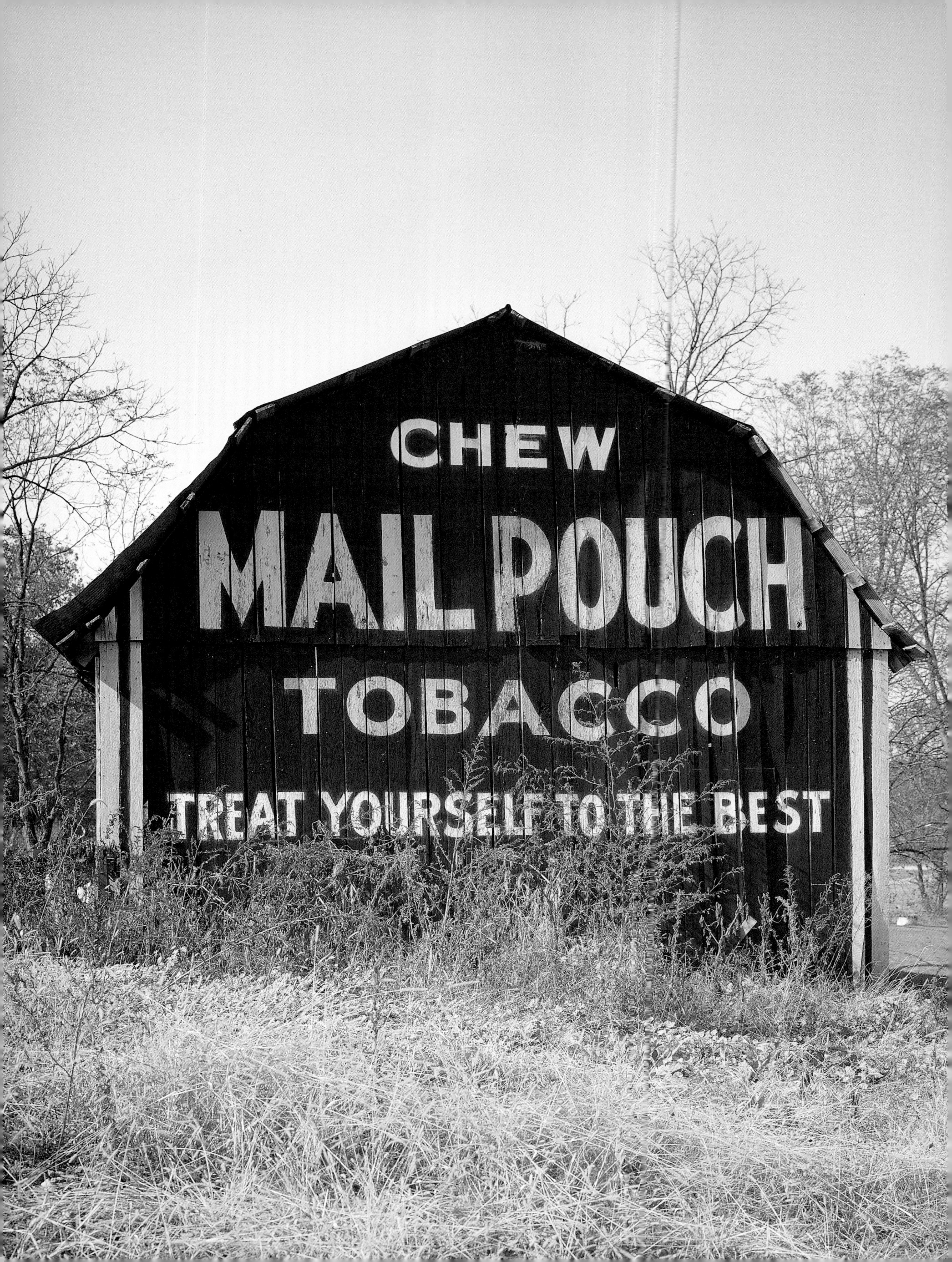
CHEW
MAIL POUCH
TOBACCO
TREAT YOURSELF TO THE BEST

Traditional and Contemporary Designs

Opposite, right, and below

On the opposite page, the barn serves as a billboard for an advertising message. The traditional image at right breathes the spirit of patriotism; Stars and Stripes and the Maple Leaf adorn many barns as well. The paintings below strike an unexpected artistic note, one old, the other new.

The Mason's Handiwork *Left and below*
Brick quoins mark the intersections of the unique seven-sided Bradley-Wheeler barn, at left, in Westport, Connecticut. It dates from 1850. Below is the old foundation of the Voorhees Farm barn in Stewartsville, New Jersey. Ventilation openings pierce the walls.

Pennsylvania Iron- and Stonework *Right and below*
A hand-forged monogram, at right, marks a time-worn stone wall in the town of Willow Street. The Lancaster barn below has strap hinges on a weathered "Dutch" (two-part) door set into a wall formed of rough and flat-faced stones wedged with "chinkers." The sand-and-limestone mortar has crumbled.

Painted Siding *Left and below*
The old oxblood-colored door at left has probably outworn several sets of hardware during its years of service on an Amish farm in Kidron, Ohio. The striking red-and-white gable of the Pennsylvania barn below has been modernized by a tier of sash windows.

Framing, Voorhees *Opposite*
The armature of the Voorhees Farm barn in Stewartsville, New Jersey, is laid bare as the building is dismantled following damage by a windstorm.

Studies in Symmetry *Opposite top and above*
On the opposite page, multipaned horizontal and vertical windows on a historic barn in Waitsfield, Vermont, form a rhythmic pattern. On the same barn (above) a double hay door comprising vertical boards graces a gable that has horizontal siding.

Vermont Dairy Barn *Left*
A Holstein-Friesian stands beside a wooden barn in Greensboro, Vermont, where dairying remains the dominant farm industry. The window, door, and paintwork detailing are typical of the region.

Frame and Log Shelters *Left and below, left*
Rough, durable pine boards form weatherproof siding on the old poultry house at left. The log barn below it, reconstructed in Upper Canada Village, Ontario, has squared timbers joined by V-notches hewed with a mortise axe.

Doors on Working Buildings *Opposite and below*
X-shaped bracing defines the barn doors on the opposite page; the example below has diagonal bracing.

Vermont Cupolas *Left and below*

The cupola is one feature that varies widely, depending upon the location and the farmer's creativity. The example at left, from Kenyon's Farm in Waitsfield, bears a monogram on each of the small gables. The one below is narrower, with a single set of louvers on each side. Vermont cupolas are usually large in proportion to the barn.

New England, Past and Present *Right and below*
The cupola at right, topped by a finial, has lost most of its
shingles and slats to the weather. It surmounts an aging barn
in Wilton, Connecticut. Below is an unusual pagoda-roofed
cupola with weather vane on a working farm in
Massachusetts.

The Reliable Weather Vane *Left and below*
The Vermont barn at left has a graceful weather vane of scrolled ironwork in the form of an arrow—one of the oldest designs for this use. Below, at left, is a traditional cow weather vane from Kenyon's Farm. The angel below strikes an original note that lends a Christmas-card effect.

A Timeless Signal *Opposite*
The bell used to call generations of workers from the fields stands ready to ring in a new day.

Glossary

auger: Tool with a spiral cutting edge for boring holes in wood

balloon framing: A type of timber framing introduced in the mid-nineteenth century, in which the studs are continuous from sill to plate

bargeboard: The board on the outside of the gable wall that runs under the edge of the roof

basilican plan: Having a central nave flanked by aisles, as in a church

batten: A narrow strip of wood

bent: Preassembled sections of timber framing

board-and-batten siding: Alternating boards and thin strips of wood (battens) used to cover a building

bow-truss roof: Semicircular wooden roof developed during the nineteenth century

brace: A diagonal timber, straight or curved, that is mortised into two timbers set at right angles to each other, to provide strength and rigidity

breeding stall: Large stall for animals giving birth to young

byre: A cow stall or cow barn

clerestory: A series of windows high in a wall

corn crib: A slatted storage container for fresh or dried corncobs

crib: A small wooden enclosure for storing grain or housing livestock or tools

cruck framing: A type of framing in which pairs of large curved timbers, or crucks, rise from ground to rooftop, serving as both posts and main rafters

cupola: A small dome or other structure on a roof

Deutsch: German word meaning "German"; sometimes anglicized to "Dutch" (in particular, "Pennsylvania Dutch")

dogtrot: A covered passageway between two parts of a building

"Dutch" door: Two-part door that allows for opening the upper and lower halves separately

flail: A free-swinging stick attached to the end of a long handle, used to thresh grain by hand

flues: Vents to carry away stale air

fretwork: Decorative panel, carving, or other openwork with interlacing designs

frow: A wedge-shaped cleaving tool

gable: The triangular wall enclosed by the sloping ends of a ridged roof

gambrel roof: Having two slopes on each side, the lower steeper than the upper

granary: Storage room or building for threshed grain

grange barn: A warehouse for harvested grain, common to monasteries and manors in the Middle Ages

hex signs: Ornamental circular paintings with geometric or natural motifs on southeastern Pennsylvania barns built by Germans

hip roof: A roof with sloping ends and sides

horreo: Spanish granary

Laube: German for "forebay," an extension of the barn floor over the lower level in a banked barn

loophole: A vertical slot in a stone wall that provides air and light

Loshoes (Long House): A connected building housing people in one section and livestock in the other

maison bloc: Breton building style in which a connected barn sheltered people, cattle, and storage areas under one roof

maison cour: Norman building style whereby separate farm buildings are grouped around a central courtyard

medieval tithe barn: Large barn of basilican plan used in medieval Europe to house grain given (tithed) to the Church or landlord

mortise: A notch cut into a piece of wood to receive a projecting part (tenon) shaped to fit

mow: Storage place for hay, usually in a loft under the roof

nogging: Any material, including stone, brick, or wattle and daub, used to fill spaces between studs

padstone: A large stone that supports a sill plate and rests immediately below a post to bear the building's weight

palisade: A protective wall of logs sharpened at one end

parapet: A low wall or railing

pentroof, pentice: A small roof over a window, door, or other opening

plate: A horizontal timber connecting the tops of the outside posts of several bents and supporting the bases of the rafters

scythe: A tool with a long blade set at an angle on a curved handle, primarily used to thresh grain

sill plates: Long horizontal timbers laid on the foundation to carry the floor joists and support the posts and studs

silo: An airtight tower in which green fodder is preserved

swing beam: A strong timber used in barn framing to support the hay mow

tenon: Projecting part cut into a piece of wood for insertion into a corresponding hole (mortise) in another piece

tip, or tilted window: A square or rectangular window set at an angle high in the gable wall of a barn

"top hat" barn: Having large projecting rain hoods over the hay doors and/or open gables

transom: Horizontal opening over doorway to admit light and air

trunnel: A wooden peg used to join two pieces of timber

wattle-and-daub construction: Made of interwoven sticks or branches covered by mud, plaster, or whitewash

wattle: Interwoven sticks or branches used for walling, fencing, and roofing

weathercock: A weather vane in the form of a rooster

whiting: Powdered chalk used in making whitewash

winnowing tray: Used in threshing grain by hand to toss it into a current of air that blows away the chaff

Index

Page numbers in bold type refer to illustrations.

Acknowledgements

The publisher would like to thank the the following individuals for their assistance in the preparation of this book: Balthazar Korab, for his inspiration and enthusiasm in addition to providing photographs as detailed below; Sara Hunt, editor; Charles Ziga, art editor and for photographs as detailed below; Nicola J. Gillies, editorial and photo research assistant and indexer; Christopher Todd Berlingo and Wendy J. Ciaccia, graphic designers; Emily Elizabeth Head, photo research assistance; Jean Ann Miller for her assistance on photographic shoots; numerous farmers and barn owners who gave their permission and assistance in the photography of their property (permission was sought and obtained wherever possible); and the following photographers, administrators, and archivists who generously helped with research: Kindra Clineff, June Griffiths, Frank Korvemaker, Ken MacCardle, Sally Morse Majewski, Sheila O'Neill of Westport Historical Society, John Sylvester, Dale Van Steenburg. Robin Langley Sommer acknowledges the invaluable research and scholarship of the authors of the following books referred to in the preparation of this volume:

Arthur, Eric, and Dudley Witney. *The Barn: A Vanishing Landmark in North America*. New York: Arrowood Press, 1989;

Endersby, Elric, et al. *Barn: The Art of a Working Building*. New York: Houghton Mifflin, 1992;

Howe, Nicholas S. *Barns*. New York: Friedman/Fairfax Publishers, 1996;

Scott, Stephen. *Amish Houses & Barns: People's Place Book No. 11*. Intercourse, Pa.: Good Books, 1991;

Sloane, Eric. *An Age of Barns*. New York: Henry Holt & Co., 1990;

———. *Our Vanishing Landscape*. New York: Ballantine Books, 1985.

Grateful acknowledgement is also made to the institutions and individuals who gave their permission to reproduce photographs, as listed below by their location in this book: © Balthazar Korab: 1, 2–3, 9, 18, 40, 43, 44t, 46b, 48b, 49, 56–57t, 60–61, 67, 70b, 72 (both), 74–75b, 76–77b, 83, 84, 85b, 91, 92, 94–95t, 95t, 96, 97 (both), 98, 100b, 100–101t, 102b, 104t & b, 111, 112t, 113, 116, 117, 118, 121, 128, 129 (all); © Charles Ziga: 4–5, 6, 7, 17, 24b, 26–27t, 27b, 30–31t, 31b, 33b, 46t, 47, 50, 52–53 (all), 58, 59, 62, 74t, 86, 87 (both), 119, 122 (both), 123 (both), 124b, 126, 127 (both), 130 (both), 131 (both), 132t, 133 (both), 134t, 135t, 136br, 137 (both), 138 (both), 139t, 140 (all) 144; © 1994 Michael A. Smith: 132b; © 1997 Kindra Clineff: 12, 16, 20–24–25t, 38–39, 120, 134–35b, 136t, 139b, 141; © Canadian Tourism Commission photo: 15 (Birgitte Nielson), 10, 69 (Alan Carruthers), 88 (Yves Beaulieu), 95b (Joseph Lederer), 109 (Yves Beaulieu), 114 (Jim Merrithew), 115t (John Devisser), 115b (Alan Carruthers), 136bl (Jim Merrithew); FPG International: 99 and 108 (© Ron Thomas), 107 (© David Noble); Hancock Shaker Village, Pittsfield, Massachusetts: 66, 78, 79; © John Sylvester: 22–23t, 32b, 34–35 (all), 65; Lehigh County Historical Society: 42, 44b, 45, 54 (both), 55, 124tl & tr, 125 (both); © NYS Department of Economic Development (1997): 11b, 24t, 36–37t, 68 (middle), 70–71t; Provincial Archives of New Brunswick: 13, 14, 64 (both), 89b; Saskatchewan Archives Board: 8 (top to bottom: R-A3900, R-A3899-1, and R-A3899-2), 90 (R-A870); Saskatchewan Government: Heritage Branch: 81 both (Frank Korvemaker), 82t (Garth Pugh), 82b (Frank Korvemaker), 93b (Garth Pugh), 102t (Frank Korvemaker), 103 (Wayne Zelmer); The Ontario Ministry of Economic Development, Trade & Tourism: 11t, 21, 23b, 26b, 48t, 51b, 57b, 68t & b, 71b, 73; Vermont Division for Historic Preservation: 19t (Sandra Cavazos), 19b (Dean Covey), 28 (both), 29, 30b, 32–33t, 36b, 37b, 75t, 76t, 80, 85t; Wisconsin Department of Tourism: 51t, 93t, 104–05b, 106 (both), 110, 112b.

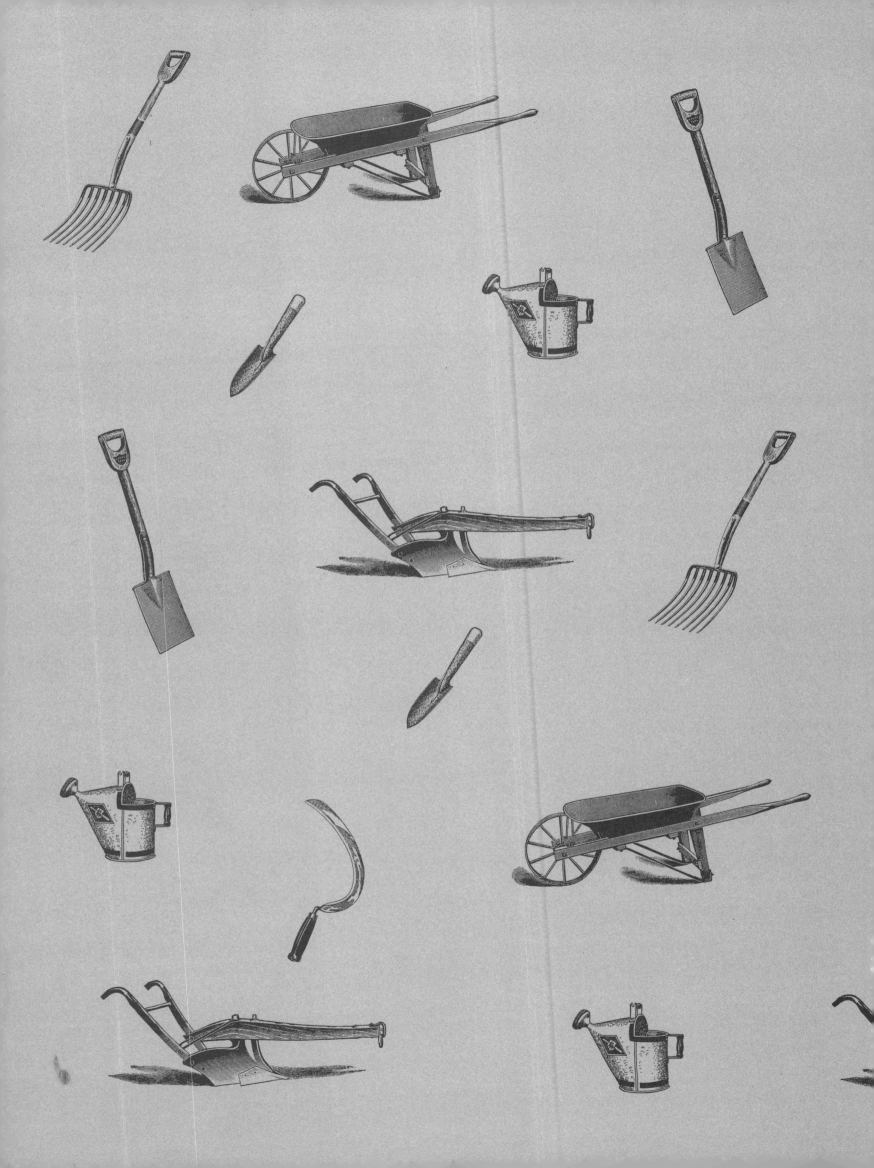